Genre | Realistic F...

Essential Question
In what ways do people show they care about each other?

Saving Stolen Treasure

by Eve Tonkin • illustrated by Merrill Rainey

Chapter 1
Stolen Treasure Is on the Rocks!

It was Friday afternoon, and play practice wasn't going well. Ms. Anderson was feeling completely worn out. Kids whirled around the room, and ideas sprang up like daisies, but no one could agree on which ones to use.

"Listen, everyone," Ms. Anderson said. "We only have two weeks until our performance!"

Some kids were still talking and shouting to express their ideas.

"King Cris, stop arguing with Queen Chelsea! Sam, please stop making that monkey noise. You are *not* going to be the monkey in the play!"

Finally some quiet fell over the room, and Ms. Anderson took a breath and continued. "We *must* decide by Monday what the treasure is going to be—Spanish gold or jewelry." A few kids started mumbling in the back. "This is serious, class. Right now, *Stolen Treasure* is on the rocks!"

The class was silent again, and Ms. Anderson smiled. "Things will be better on Monday," she said. "I, for one, am looking forward to going with my husband to the swing dancing championships on Saturday. Have a good weekend, everyone!"

To the class's surprise, Mr. Kowalski, a substitute teacher, was in the classroom on Monday morning. "Ms. Anderson broke her leg dancing," he told them.

"Oh, no!" Erica exclaimed. "When will she be back?"

"I don't know," Mr. Kowalski said. "But I do know we need to get started with play practice."

"Only if I can play a monkey," Sam chimed in. Everyone groaned.

Rani muttered, "Just as long as I don't have to wear that stupid hat."

"You have to wear the hat," objected Violet. "Don't be fussy."

"Ms. Anderson says you need to decide what the treasure is going to be," said Mr. Kowalski.

"Jewelry!" shouted several kids.

"Spanish coins!" said others.

"Settle down!" said Mr. Kowalski. "I can see that I will need to talk to Ms. Anderson before we can continue. So everyone take out your reading."

Chelsea and Erica looked at each other in dismay. "We're wasting precious time," Chelsea whispered.

Erica's gaze strayed to the class portraits on the wall. It was Ms. Anderson's idea to take everyone's photo on the last field trip. "We need Ms. Anderson's advice. Let's visit her after school," she whispered back.

STOP AND CHECK

Why does the class have a substitute teacher?

Chapter 2
Working Together

On Tuesday afternoon, Erica and Chelsea went to Ms. Anderson's house. Ms. Anderson lived next door to Erica. She'd known Ms. Anderson long before she became her student. Mr. Anderson answered the door.

"Hi, Mr. Anderson," Erica said. "How is Ms. Anderson?"

"Not that great," Mr. Anderson replied. "She's been worried since the substitute teacher called to say that the play wasn't going well."

"We can't do it without her," Chelsea replied.

"Unfortunately, you'll have to," Mr. Anderson said. "She won't be coming back to school for a few months."

"Can we please see her?" Chelsea asked.

"I'm sure she would love that. I'll let her know you're here."

"We can't ask Ms. Anderson for advice now," Erica whispered to Chelsea as soon as he had gone. "We need to cheer her up, not make her worry even more!"

It was strange to see Ms. Anderson with her leg in a cast and piled high on pillows. "Don't look so worried!" she said to the girls. "I'm enjoying the rest."

"We brought you a get-well card," said Erica, opening her backpack.

"That's very thoughtful, Erica," said Ms. Anderson. "How's everything going?"

"Play practice was tough at first," Erica said, "but it's getting better."

"That's great news!" exclaimed Ms. Anderson.

The next day in class, Mr. Kowalski announced, "Erica and Chelsea have something to say before we start."

"We went to see Ms. Anderson after school yesterday," Erica told everyone. "She won't be coming back for quite a while."

Everyone started talking at once.

"How big is her cast?" called Sam.

"It's huge," said Chelsea. "Her whole leg is in the cast. And she has to keep it elevated."

"That must be uncomfortable," said Violet.

"What about the play?" asked Michael. "Are we still going to do it?"

"That's what we need to talk about," said Erica firmly.

She continued, "Ms. Anderson really cares about us doing a good job with the play. She's worried that we won't be able to pull it off without her."

"No wonder, with all our arguing and stuff," said Michael.

"Exactly," said Erica. "We've got to cooperate and start listening to one another. We owe it to Ms. Anderson to make this play awesome!"

"Who agrees with Erica?" Michael asked, looking around.

Everyone's hand was raised.

"Great!" said Erica. "It's unanimous. Now, what should we work on first?"

"For a start, Sam, you can be the king's tiger, *not* another monkey," Violet said.

Sam nodded.

"And no more arguing about the treasure," Chelsea added. "Let's vote on it now."

"I have another idea," said Jaden. "Why don't we have coins *and* jewelry? That way, everyone gets what they want."

"Yes!" everyone replied in chorus. "Let's have both!"

"Let's write the part about the treasure into the play now," Violet said. "Then the writing will be finished."

"That's a good idea," Mr. Kowalski replied. "You guys are on a roll now!"

Why do the two girls take over running the class play?

Chapter 3

Opening Night

On opening night, Ms. Anderson couldn't wait to see the play. According to the latest reports from Mr. Kowalski and Erica, her class had done a great job of working together.

Ms. Anderson whispered in Mr. Anderson's ear. "Could you please go backstage? Tell the class that they don't have to break a leg because I already did it. Their success is guaranteed!"

Mr. Anderson nodded. He went backstage and came back a few minutes later, giving Ms. Anderson the thumbs-up.

The lights dimmed, and the audience settled down.

Onstage the class was having a fantastic time. Their good ideas had taken root and grown into a magnificent tree, heavy with stories and wondrous to climb.

Everyone's ideas had helped to make the play about a stolen treasure better.

The class had fun working together, too. King Cris and Queen Chelsea stopped fighting. Erica helped Sam get ready for his role as a tiger.

Best of all, the treasure of Spanish gold and jewelry worked perfectly. It sparkled in the bright stage lights.

Suddenly the play was over, and it was time to join hands onstage and take a bow. The audience members leaped to their feet, clapping, stomping, and cheering. Ms. Anderson cheered loudest of all.

Erica gave the signal, and the fourth-graders began to chant, "Ms. An-der-son! Ms. An-der-son!"

Mr. Anderson helped his surprised wife up onto the stage. Her class encircled her as King Cris and Queen Chelsea presented her with a bouquet.

Ms. Anderson took the microphone. "I'm so proud of my wonderful class tonight," she began, her voice full of emotion. "They wrote the play themselves, and then I went and broke my leg. It wasn't always easy, but they really pulled together!"

Everyone exchanged proud smiles as another round of applause shook the auditorium.

STOP AND CHECK

Why did the class call Ms. Anderson up onto the stage?

Respond to Reading

Summarize

Use the most important details from *Saving Stolen Treasure* to summarize the story. Your graphic organizer may help you.

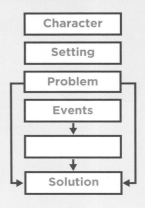

Text Evidence

1. How is *Saving Stolen Treasure* an example of realistic fiction? Use details from the story to explain. GENRE

2. What problem is the class having at the beginning of the story? PROBLEM AND SOLUTION

3. What does the simile "ideas sprang up like daisies" on page 2 mean? SIMILES AND METAPHORS

4. Write about Erica's problem in the story and how she solved it. WRITE ABOUT READING

Compare Texts

Read about a boy who helped his sister overcome her shyness.

Miguel's Amazing Shyness Cure

Miguel aimed the basketball at the hoop.

"Hey, Miguel!" Cody called. "Your sister's here again!"

Jade was standing at the side of the basketball court, looking small and sad.

Miguel walked over to his sister. "What's up?" he asked her gently. "Why aren't you playing with the kids in your class?" Jade's cheeks reddened, and she kicked a pebble.

Miguel knew that it was tough for Jade being shy. It was especially hard now that Sarah, Jade's best friend, had moved away.

Miguel felt sorry for Jade, but he also felt annoyed. These days, she hung around him all the time. "I'll walk you back to class," he said.

After school, Miguel met Jade in front of the school.

"This is for you," she said, handing him a picture. "We had to draw our best friend, so I drew a picture of you shooting hoops."

Miguel admired the picture. "It's awesome," he said, smiling at her.

At home, Mom was making Jade's favorite dessert to cheer her up. "If only I could give her something to cure her shyness," Miguel thought.

Suddenly he had an idea!

Illustration: Joanne Renaud

"I have an announcement," Miguel said later that night at dinner. "Jade gave me a drawing today, and I have something for her."

He handed her a box with MIGUEL'S AMAZING SHYNESS CURE written on it.

Jade opened the lid. Miguel's favorite azurite crystal lay inside.

"It helped me when I was shy," he explained. "You carry it in your pocket, and when you feel shy, you squeeze it, take a deep breath, and your shyness goes away."

"Wow! Thanks, Miguel!" Jade said, her eyes shining. "I can't wait to try it tomorrow!"

Make Connections

How do Miguel's actions show that he cares about his sister? ESSENTIAL QUESTION

How are Erica in *Saving Stolen Treasure* and Miguel in *Miguel's Amazing Shyness Cure* alike? TEXT TO TEXT

Illustration: Joanne Renaud

Focus on

Genre

Realistic Fiction Realistic fiction tells a story that could be true. Writers use believable characters and settings, and the plots usually involve the kinds of problems that many of us have. As readers, we can identify with the characters and their problems almost as if we knew them ourselves.

Read and Find In *Saving Stolen Treasure,* Erica's problem is to make the class play a success. Does that seem believable to you? In *Miguel's Amazing Shyness Cure*, Miguel's little sister follows him around because she's shy and hasn't made new friends. Does that seem believable to you?

Your Turn

Compare yourself with one of the characters from either story. Think about the ways you are similar and different. What is another problem the character might have to face? What would you do if you were in his or her shoes? Turn to a partner and discuss the character you chose to compare yourself with. How did your characters resolve the problems you gave them? Are your problems and solutions believable?